50 Lessons

In 50 Years

50 Lessons

In 50 Years

By Dea A. Myers

1st Edition

2026

Thanks

To God, The Father, The Son and Spirit. It doesn't matter what I do, I will never be able to thank You enough for all your love, goodness and blessings.

To my kiddos, your support means the world to me. To Chris, thanks for being on the boat with me.

To all my family, friends and supporters, thank you.

"His name is Emmanuel because He is always with us."

Dea A. Myers

50 Lessons in 50 Years

-A Brief Introduction-

Since last year I have thought about some things I would like to share with others, things I have learned living the life God gave me. Recently a friend told me I should have a podcast because she likes my insights and advice, and I am not a podcast person, but I love writing, so why not do it?

Another motivation for me writing this book is that when I was a kid I loved listening to older people. It was as if I could get a shortcut instead of going through the long, hard and painful road. When I listened to them I was a child, but I am turning 50 myself and now I am the one who has walked by a path many haven't. Now it is my time to share with people what I have learned so far.

This book is not about telling people about what life is like as we already have the Bible to tell us what life is like. But it is more like mental notes that usually keep pondering in my mind and I think it could be good if shared.

I am also doing this for my kids. I wanted them to learn from my experiences and have the best life possible while they are in this world.

As a writer I don't believe there is not a better way to celebrate my 50's than this, by doing what I love the most, which is writing and inspiring people.

This book is about faith, life, lessons and love.

Welcome to this new journey,

Dea A. Myers

1. There's Only One of You in This World

One of the things I've learned which has changed my perspective about myself and the world is that we are unique. This is actually one of the coolest truths in this world. God made only one of us. There are no copies, and no duplicates. We are unique, and He made sure we knew this when He put a unique DNA chain inside each one of us.

Scientists have made a lot of progress on deciphering it, but there is still so much unknown information inside our DNA that is absolutely impressive.

"Oh, I already know this." We may say, but what I question myself is *if we really know that.*

When I think about God creating us I think of a scientist creating each one of us, and choosing the best combinations from our parents genes and relatives, using the best combinations to create each one of us. When I think about this, I also think of an artist placing the right tones and colors in the right place, so everything is going to be beautiful as He dreamed. All recorded in detail on our DNA chain.

I imagine Him giving us a unique soul and heart. You are not just one in the crowd, and you are not just a number; you were fearfully and wonderfully made in the image of God.

When circumstances try to put you down, remember there is only one of you in this world. Nobody can be you, nobody can replace you and you are extremely valuable for God.

2. We All Matter

Another important truth I discovered in my life is that as individuals we are unique, valuable and special, but as humans we are all valuable and *we all* matter to God.

This should be a simple truth but it is not because our society is built on comparisons. This world's standard of success is about beauty, money and status. Do you know the scary part about this? They can all fade in a blink of an eye. Posting the wrong thing on social media? There it goes your influence. Put your money in the wrong investment? There it goes your money. Wrinkles are showing despite all your aesthetical procedures? There it goes your beauty and youth at the same time.

Many people have not even had the chance to be on the top of the mountain. Think about that. Every day we are rejected because we are not "too" of something or "not enough" of something else.

You may be rejected because you are too young or too old, because you are too heavy or because you are too thin. You may be rejected because you are overqualified or not qualified enough. You may be rejected because of your ethnicity, race, economical status, age, personality traits, physical appearance and the list goes on.

But God loves humanity as a whole. Every day He sends the sun to warm us up, and the rain to make the plants grow, He makes sure your body continues working. He sent His Son for all. When Jesus healed and blessed people, there were no conditions with it, He helped all and blessed all because He loved all of them.

So when people try to put you down, try to remember you are not *less* than anyone. For God, you are just as important as anyone else.

3. A Unique Journey

We all matter to God and all individuals are unique. However, since nobody is like you, your journey in this world is also unique. Since our birth, our journey has been unlike anyone else's. Yes, as being part of the human race and having some similarities, our story may look similar to someone else's, but despite the likenesses, your story is one of a kind and it will remain like this until your last breath.

Sometimes I like to imagine that our story is like a book written by God, in which we are the main character. He is the author, the one who brings the supporting characters, the circumstances, the joys, the sadness, the challenges and surprises. Each day we are in this world, we build a new page with God and people around us- one more page of this unique and amazing book. Can you imagine God's library? It must be beautiful, don't you think?

Some of us had the perfect childhood, while others- a traumatic childhood; some had golden teenage years, of being popular, building memorable years, but others had the most confusing and turbulent teen years. Some of us were born knowing what profession to follow when growing up, and others are still seeking a profession they can identify with. Some stayed married, others went through divorce, some had kids; others didn't. Some had aged well, others haven't.

This life is yours so it is the story of your life. Nobody in this world can have your life, the same way you cannot have someone else's life. No one can walk in your shoes and follow your journey. This is the beauty of life. This is your path, even with your mistakes and flaws or your accomplishments. Learn to value your story. Learn with your mistakes and rejoice with your victories. Don't be ashamed of your story because God can use it for His glory. Remember you are not alone on this road. God is beside you in this journey.

4. There Isn't Overcoming Without Challenges

Imagine you were a child who had a perfect childhood. Imagine you never had to deal with bullying, had loving and sweet parents, the best friends at school and all the toys you desired.

Now imagine if you also had a perfect adolescence. Your body looked like Barbie and you had an amazing boyfriend like Ken. Imagine there were no gossips, your friends were amazing, and zero drama. You had no trouble with math or any other subject. You were never shy making school presentations, but you were also good at sports with a lot of trophies and medals to show from it. You went to the mall with a limitless credit card and you were able to buy all the clothes a teen has always dreamed of, eat fast food and never put on an ounce. (Wow! That's the dream, isn't it?)

Imagine you became an adult and already knew what you wanted to be and be easily accepted at the University of your Dreams. Your college years would be fantastic and, after you graduate, you would already have the job waiting for you. On the elevator you meet the person of your dreams who you go on to marry and have the perfect wedding ceremony, such as the honeymoon and the relationship.

You wouldn't have a single issue during your pregnancy- no swollen feet, morning sickness, or heartburns. You wouldn't feel any pain during the labor. You "sneeze" during the labor and the baby would be here. Your kids would grow polite and obedient and you would go through menopause without any issues.

Wow! Just wow! Imagine if this was your life. Wouldn't it be amazing? Everything worked the entire time. But, if this was your life, do you know what you would have learned? This, I can answer you: Absolutely nothing.

We all desire a perfect life. We dread our challenges and difficulties. We get upset with God because life is not working the way we expect and ask God why we are going through difficulties. But, we forget the difficult moments are the moments which shape us. God uses the challenges to make us grow, to thicken our skin or to soften us up, depending on what we need.

When I look back on my life I see so many happy and beautiful moments, but I also see moments of struggles and difficulties. These moments were so hard, but they shaped the person I am today and I am thankful for it.

It doesn't matter how life is portrayed on social media, the truth is nobody has a perfect life. We all have difficulties and we all struggle in different ways, but God uses these moments for our growth, for His glory and for deepening our relationship with Him.

5. We Need To Get Away from What Makes Us Sin

In the Bible Jesus tells us if our hands make us sin we need to cut them off. And surely He was not talking specifically about our hands, but from everything which makes us sin and leads us away from the Lord. Such as a person who struggles with alcohol going to a party. Is he or she strong enough to be in that place or situation?

There are some things in this world that mess with us which are called weaknesses. Do you know those things which lead us to sin? Sometimes we are not strong enough or have enough self control to handle them.

Jesus knows this. That's why He told us we need to get away from such things. When we talk about weaknesses, we usually think about alcohol, drugs and immorality, and this is correct, but sometimes we forget relationships may also lead us to sin.

Many kids tried drugs or alcohol for the first time due to a friend. It seemed fun, light, simple, but sometimes they can get in this situation and it can be hard to get out of it.

What about relationships in general? I've lost count of the number of people I have met who worked in the church, were dedicated to the Lord, happy people with sparkling eyes and a big smile who changed completely because of a person they were friends with or were romantically involved with.

Healthy relationships help you to keep walking and building your life, but unhealthy relationships are like a hamster wheel where you run, run, but you don't get anywhere. It is sad to see people who were so full of life and light becoming dark and oppressed. They stopped going to the church, serving God, and distanced themselves from family and friends. They are slowly destroyed by a relationship that is not adding anything, but taking away from them.

Healthy relationships bring us joy and peace, but unhealthy relationships are the opposite. When we think about getting away from things that lead you to sin, we usually think about alcohol and other things, but this chapter is talking about everything that makes you sin, including relationships.

In general, people are such a blessing to us, a real present from God, but sometimes some people may be like a trap from the enemy to steal our joy, take away our peace and destabilize us. If you are strong enough to deal with it, if God told you to stay around, do it. However, if this relationship is leading you away from the Lord and loved ones, and if it is transforming you

into a vengeful and anguished person you may rethink
the relationship.

6. Love and Having a Relationship Are Two Different Things.

I don't know where or when this started, but, at a certain point, we confused things a little bit. Yes, Jesus wants us to have a cordial relationship with our fellow humans. God tells us in the Bible we need to love people as we love ourselves. We need to treat other people with the utmost regard, and we need to live in peace with people around us as much as we can. We need to serve people, care about people, help people, but there is no place in the Bible God is telling you that you need to have a relationship with everyone.

I have seen multiple people submit themselves to all levels of toxicity in relationships because, "God told us we need to love people." Hey, this is true, we need to love people but we are not obligated to have a deep relationship with them. Relationships demand trust, respect, mutual love and consideration.

Love someone and have a relationship with someone are two distinct things. First, it is impossible to have a deep relationship with everyone. We are limited by time and space. We can't be everywhere all the time.

So, it means you are going to connect with some people on a deeper level than others and the same is going to happen with others too.

God wants you to love people. It means you can love the person, pray for the person, serve the person, help the person, care about the person, but you don't necessarily need to have a relationship for it to happen. Relationships are like a present, a privilege for those you trust and really want to share life with.

And I say this because many times I was around people who treated me poorly because I thought I had to have a relationship with that person because of God. And this is so ingrained in us that right now people are having trouble digesting this, but it is true. God wants you to love people. He is not obligating you to be in a deep relationship with them.

7. We Can't Control People

This is one of the hardest truths of this life. We can't control people. If we don't understand this, we may become frustrated and bitter.

Let's suppose you found your dream job. You are so excited about that job- the pay is good and it is a good career opportunity, but when you get there you find out your boss is not how you expected them to be, or some of your coworkers are hard to work with. I have seen people getting sick because of their work environment. In a situation like this you have a couple choices: you get a new job, you stand up for yourself or you learn to deal with this.

The same thing happens with relationships as well. We create these long term plans in our minds, including other people, but you can't control the outcome of many things. For example, when you marry someone, while you are dating, so many promises are made, but real life happens in a different way.

Let's suppose when you marry, you both agreed to exercise together after work, but after marriage your spouse doesn't care about it. You may talk and complain, but you cannot force the person to exercise with you. So, you can go yourself, which would be frustrating, I understand, and if it is something that bothers you a lot, you can seek counseling, but truth is, you can only control what you can do, not your spouse.

The same happens with kids. Oh, when we are pregnant, isn't it amazing?! We create all these expectations about our children and how they are going to be, but when they are born we meet our real child. They are going to be cute, the most beautiful kids, but, believe me, motherhood is very humbly. You will see your kids doing things you absolutely never imagined they would.

Like the day I saw my toddler messing up with the offering plate at the church, he jumped from a chair, while I was in the choir, and punched the pastor's buttocks. I wanted to die right there of embarrassment. How did this happen again? Thank goodness that church was so loving and kind; they laughed and said the kids were like this, full of energy.

Or the day my son started running nonstop in a grocery store and literally, the whole family was running after him. When we finally reached him, a customer came to us, laughing hysterically and said we looked like those families in the movies, running in the airport to catch the plane. I smiled, being polite, but in my mind I was asking him, "Do you have kids?"

So being a mom is very humbly since you will quickly realize you didn't birth a robot, but a human being. You can't control your kids every single second of the day. You can only deal with who they are, with their virtues and flaws.

And the same happens with singles. Every person they meet, every new dinner, every new conversation there is this hope that this may be the right person. Sometimes you are getting so excited with someone, but the person suddenly changes and you feel disappointed because once again, we can't control what people do or how they feel, etc.

I know it can be hard, but on a side note, I have learned so many lessons in my life dealing with people. It is hard, but not pointless. God will use our disappointments to teach us to be humble, respect other people, and accept different outcomes. It leads us to fix situations, compromise in what we can, and make agreements, when possible, in order to coexist in peace. It is a rich process towards our growth as Christians and as humans too.

8. Your Feelings Matter

My whole lifetime I heard things like, "Don't pay attention to your feelings. Do things in a rational way," etc... I understand our decisions must come from a place where we have to analyze our actions. In other words, we need to think and ponder things before acting, but our feelings *should not* be ignored.

Have you heard the expression "gut feeling?" Like when you feel something is not right and your body signals this to you? I not only believe this exists, but I also believe this is stronger in Christians since we have the Holy Spirit and He can see things we can't.

When I was in my thirties, I really fell in love with a guy. But every time we went out, as much as I liked him and wanted to be with him, I felt physically sick as if there was a ball in the middle of my stomach.

I remember this dinner specifically because it was perfect. Nothing crazy happened. The weather was good, not too hot, not too cold, the food was delicious, the tire didn't pop on the way, and it didn't rain cats and dogs, but the knot in the middle of my stomach just didn't go away. It turns out he was a good person and there was nothing wrong with him, but we were not meant to be together.

These things seem to be little and irrelevant, because people tell you to live rationally. There was nothing wrong with it rationally, but this feeling was telling me there was something wrong. When these things happen, we really need to pray and ask God what is going on.

I have come to know so many people who ignored these signs and they ended up getting into a bad situation. So, if you have these uneasy feelings about something, do not be afraid to ask God about it because God knows things about the future you don't.

9. You Have to Deal with Your Feelings

If you are a human being, you are going to hurt and you are going to be hurt. None of us like to be hurt, to be disappointed by someone, neglected etc, but we need to deal with these feelings before they damage our own life or someone else's life.

Envy was the feeling that made Joseph's brothers sell him as a slave. Self-sufficiency was the feeling that made Peter stop looking to Jesus and start sinking when he was walking on the water. Rejection was the feeling that moved Cain to hurt his own brother. Greed was the feeling that moved Absalom to pursue the kingdom of his own father, and lust was what moved Amnon to abuse his own sister.

Before sin happened, there was a feeling growing and spreading. The main question is, how are we going to deal with these feelings? Many people deal with this in different ways. Some seek counseling, some psychiatrists, and just to be clear, I am not against it, as it is a blessing to have a good therapist, but what has worked for me is to seek God's healing.

I pray a lot for God to heal my heart, to remove anger, resentment, etc. So far it has worked. I keep praying until that bad feeling is not there anymore.

Prayers are free, accessible, you don't need an appointment to talk to God and they are effective since, according to the Bible, God is our maker. No one can fix something better than its maker. All we have to do is to be really honest to God and open our hearts to Him.

Our feelings may be dealt or they may grow in a negative way. In a way or another, we need to deal with these feelings before they take a bad turn.

10. We Are Not Enough

One day my kid came from school with a bracelet saying "I am enough" and it devastated me. As much as I know the teachers are trying to teach the kids to not rely on other children to be happy and be content with themselves, I know this bracelet is far from Biblical. This is because Christianity is about community, a big family, and a body in which Jesus is the head.

In a very subtle way we are being taught we are enough but this is not the truth. The truth is actually the opposite, we all need one another. You had a good and productive day today because someone made the bread you had for breakfast. Someone drove a truck and filled the gas pumps so you could fill your car to go to work. You had a good day today because someone showed up to work at the electric company and is making sure you have energy to work while your child can be at school for the same reason.

See? Just in a couple examples I am showing you how much we rely on one another. Can you imagine if these people didn't show up? You would have to wake up way early in the morning to make bread from scratch. How would you get gas if the gas pump wasn't filled? How would you be able to work without power? How would you be able to send your kid to school without gas and electricity?

We all need one another. We are not enough. God's design is for us to live in community, and not a self-centered and self-sufficient lifestyle.

11. We All Need a Village

There is a popular African saying you need a village to raise a child. It means mom and dad are not enough. A child needs grandparents, friends, neighbors, aunts, uncles, etc. The same happens with us. I have been around for some time and I can guarantee that people are getting more and more socially isolated as time goes on.

"I don't need anyone because, you know, I have the internet, I have streaming TV and a microwave. People are horrible and I am fine by myself." If people could be brutally honest, we would listen to something like this, but this culture of isolation weakens our society in so many ways that it is hard to put into words.

Bottom line what is behind "I am fine by myself" is selfishness. I don't want to be burdened with people's problems. But have you thought you could be in trouble one day too?

Can you imagine if, God forbid, you get into a car accident? Can you imagine if you break a leg? Who is going to help you? Can you imagine those people whose homes were washed away during the last floods? They lost their cars and homes. Where are they going to live? What are they going to wear? How are they going to get to work?

Yesterday I saw a dad on a podcast proudly saying his kids don't need any sociability and it broke me. We are so far from what God designed. We are locked inside our homes, living in a self-centered lifestyle and we forget God wants us to cry and laugh with one another. We should carry each others' burdens so life may be lighter to us. This is the way God wants us to live.

I wish I could tell you there is an easy and totally safe way to do this, but there isn't. I wish I could tell you that all the people around you have good intentions and a good heart, but I can't. Many times this will be the case but other times it won't. There are people who will try to take advantage of you, and people who will break your heart. So I get you, it is hard, but we do have the Holy Spirit. We can pray for direction, and ask Him to reveal what is going on with people around us.

We need to be prudent without giving up on people since we can be a blessing for so many and vice versa. When we live in a community someone will show up for you. That's the principle of a community. I help you and you help me. A little help makes a big difference.

12. It Is Okay To Not Be Okay.

Another thing I have learned in this life is that *it is okay to not be okay*. Many times we feel this pressure to smile all the time, to be fine all the time, but we all go through issues or difficulties. Sometimes it is one punch after another and you feel discouraged. The faith heroes in the Bible also had a bad time, as sometimes they felt lost, but they never lost their faith. They were discouraged, and they were sad but they never stopped believing God could change their circumstances.

I consider myself a bubbly, happy person, but I have my days like everyone else. On days like these, I pray, read the Word, worship, watch encouraging sermons, but mostly, I stay still. Sometimes you just need to listen to God; you just need to open your eyes and your ears to your surroundings so you can process what is going on.

It is so important to be still and listen to God. This world is so noisy, so loud and we are always so busy we can't pay attention. So I take this time to ask God what He is trying to tell me and ask Him to teach me what I need to learn. I am not depressed or I am not feeling hopeless, I am just seeking for the One who has the answers I need.

13. Prayer Works

One of the most powerful things I have learned in this life is that **prayers work**. I actually have learnt this from a very young age. I remember when I was 10 I was having swimming lessons and they were having a competition. I wanted a gold medal so much. I had spent the whole week prior to the date praying for it. I remember getting there, getting in my position and waiting for the next competitors to show up. Nobody did. So the officials came to me and told me I had to swim by myself. I was so nervous I swam like a crazy person. People were booing me, and my brother was so embarrassed of my performance, he pretended he didn't know me, but I finished it and guess what? I got my golden medal!

At that time, I felt so bad for receiving that medal, but today, I wish I could have kept it. It was the first miracle I can recall. Truth is I was so bad at swimming the only way I could earn the medal was if nobody showed up.

Miracles are not about someone who deserves it, but about a Father who wants to give a present to His child and I can guarantee you I have seen many miracles from God.

The Bible says all we have to do is to ask and it shall be given to you. All your kids need to do to get something from you is to ask, isn't it? It is the same with our Heavenly Father. When we pray in the name of Jesus we touch God's heart in a very special way.

14. Persevering in Prayer

Another lesson I have learned about prayer is you **need to persevere on it**. Sometimes people tell me they don't know if prayers work because they have prayed for something for some time and it didn't happen. Two months and they give up.

What if I tell you I have prayed nonstop for a friend for more than two years? This girl, who had been so desperate for two years, so many times thought about ending with it all and now is living exactly what I asked for, a new life. She has this big smile as she is so happy. God has been so generous with her. It is beautiful to see the Lord changing lives in such a powerful way. So I've learned to not give up praying for a cause, unless God tells me to do so.

15. A Couple Lessons about Prayer

Still about prayer I learned a couple of other things…
One, **you need to believe you can receive it**. If you ask
God for something, but in your heart you doubt it, it
may not happen. Two, **sometimes what we ask is not
aligned with God's plan for us or His kingdom**. And we
need to trust He knows things we don't.

For example, let's suppose you are praying to move to a
certain city or part of the country, but God is not done
yet with you in the place you are living in. He still has
things to teach you there and He still wants to use you
in this city you are living in. So if God does what you
want, you are going to miss what He wants to teach you
and you are going to miss the opportunity to serve Him
where you are.

Basically, God is inclined to give us what we ask. This is
the reality, but if He says "no" it is not because He
doesn't care, but because has a reason for it.

16. Time is Life

One of the things I have learned is that ***time is life-*** what you are doing with your time you are doing to your life. Time is not money as they say, time is life. The way you spend your time determines how you are spending your life.

Think about Jesus. He went to weddings, had a great time with people around Him, but while on Earth Jesus didn't waste a second of His life. He sought for the presence of His Father, He helped people, connected with them and blessed them.

I know we have bills to pay, a house to clean, kids to take care of, work to do, but in our free time, what are we doing? Are we seeking God? Are we connecting with people? Are we blessing people? Are we spending time with the ones we love? What are we doing with our time? We need to be good stewards with the time we have.

17. God Has His Own Time

I have always loved art in many forms and I have always loved to listen to comedians. I have always loved comedy movies, shows, soap operas, etc. It is so amazing to make people laugh, right? I always thought being a comedian was a natural gift, and I am not saying comedians do not have this natural talent, but comedy turns out to be something which needs to be well planned for it to work.

It means in order for people to laugh, you have to be in the right place, doing the right facial expressions and saying the right things. This needs to be really rehearsed between actors and performers, because one wrong movement and the laughter is not going to happen, one wrong movement and the pie will be just a pie with no amusing effect.

God knows how the right time is important. He is a perfectionist. Look at the sky, the shapes of the clouds, the sparkle of the stars and the different types of birds He created. Everything He created has its right time. If the sun comes out later, it will influence so many things on the planet. Everything has a right time to happen and this also applies to our lives.

Imagine you've met a person and you like that person romantically, you pray for the person, but it doesn't happen. You become disappointed and frustrated, thinking God doesn't love you, doesn't answer your prayers, but the truth is God has your best interest. The person may not be right person, but it also may be the right person in the wrong time. Sometimes the person is not ready for you or vice versa, and if this relationship happens now, it will be a disaster. God doesn't want that.

He loves you. He wants the best for you, but for God's best to happen it needs to be in the right time. The same thing is applicable to our careers, parenthood, etc. There is a right time for everything. Waiting is about trusting in God's love for us.

18. Feed Your Brain

One of the things I discovered is that **our brain needs to be fed too**. "Oh Dea, I read the Bible." The Bible is certainly a book that challenges our thinking, but the Bible is also our bread, our spiritual "Superfood." If you are a Christian, you are supposed to be reading the Bible. This is Christianity 101 for you. It will challenge your brain and bring you comfort, while teaching you about the Lord.

However, the same way our body needs to be fed, our minds need it too. I know we need to be careful with what we read so it will be a blessing and not a waste of time, but there are plenty of interesting books that will bring us interesting information, new vocabulary and stimulate our train of thought.

Reading is also good for our emotional and mental state. It helps to be more empathetic, to get away from our daily routine and to think about topics that are around us.

I know as a mom reading something beyond the Bible and kids' homework may be tough, but even if you take one or two pages a day it can make a difference. You will feel your brain is alive, not dormant or numb.

19. A Resting Time

One of the things I have learned in my life is to do everything I can to **honor a resting day**. Some people rest and worship on Saturdays, some on Sundays, some have to work on both days and have a day off in the middle of the week, so that has to be their day of rest, but I have learned how important it is to set aside this time. Jesus said in the Bible the Sabbath, the day of rest, wasn't created because of God, but because of men. In other words, God doesn't need to rest. We do.

Honoring this commandment sometimes is not easy. Your brain is usually so accelerated with a never ending "to do list" it is hard to just sit and do nothing. I have come to realize the weekends I rest, I have more energy during the following week. The opposite happens when I do not rest as I spend the following week exhausted.

20. Let Them Know They Are Loved

As a parent, I have come to realize there is nothing more important than **giving your children the assurance they are loved.** When I say "love", I am not saying you have to do everything they want. You have to be firm sometimes. You have to teach and educate them, but always give them the assurance they are loved.

I've come to see adults dealing with insecurities and lack of confidence because they were never sure their parents loved them. If your child does not have this assurance, they will have difficulties in relationships, and may have trouble to give and receive love, because in their minds, how can they be loved if their parents haven't loved them? How can they give love if they are not sure they ever received it?

Assuring your kids you love them won't make you look weak or look as if you are losing your authority. It will just create in your child's heart a blanket of love they know they can hold on. Whatever happens in the world, they have the assurance someone loves them. In darker days, it is something we all need. The assurance we are loved.

21. Let them Grow

Let your kids grow. I know it is scary. They were just babies shortly ago. But guess what? They are not babies anymore. They can do things they couldn't before and it is time to let them grow.

One of the great pleasures I have in life is to help my kids with their projects. It is special that they have a project, even if it is to build a cardboard rocket ship. It is so important for us to see them learning and growing and at the same time allowing us to be part of their dreams and plans. I know it seems to be one more thing in your list to do, but helping your kids to develop their abilities and helping your kids blossom should be one of the most important items on your list. We are not raising a forever kid. We are raising the future adults of our society.

22. The Most Important Decision of Your Life

As a Christian, the most important decision one can make is to follow Christ. It is to commit to Him and His principles. It is to repent and ask for forgiveness when we do wrong and to seek Him in order to do right.

When we accept Christ, we receive special life changing presents from God that will change our lives forever. First of all, we will be reconciled with God the Father, our creator and sustainer. Second of all, we will be saved. We are welcomed into God's family and I can't state enough how special this is. If I go to Japan today and go to a Christian service, I know I will be home. Third of all, according to the Bible, those who accept Christ will live forever.

Also, when we accept Christ we receive presents to help us to navigate this world. His Word, also called the Bible, is a collection of 66 books in which we can learn about God- The Father, The Son and The Holy Spirit. It is also a book, which helps us to find guidance for our lives and the promises God made for us. We also receive the

Holy Spirit, who will be within us, giving us direction and assisting us in all sorts of ways.

So, if you are a Christian, this is the most important decision of your life.

23. Nothing Without Christ

As a Christian, I have learned in this life I can't do anything without Christ. One of the most powerful verses of Scripture for me is when Jesus says "Without me you can't do anything." I apply this in everything I do in my life. Why? Because I've tried this before. I tried to love people before on my own strength and I failed, I tried to forgive people on my own strength and guess what, failed again. I tried to become a better person and I have to admit I failed.

Everything changed for me when I understood without Jesus I can't do anything. This was a turning point for me. I found the secret of living a good Christian life and it was right before me. So now if I need to forgive someone I ask Jesus to help me to do it through His Spirit. If I need to love someone and it is hard, I ask Jesus. This is the key. We can't do anything without Christ.

I know it seems simple, but I became a better person when I started doing it. I started to love more and forgive more. Jesus grew inside of me while my own flesh became smaller. Am I perfect? Far from it, I am still a sinner, but yet I forgive and love more than I did before. This happened simply because I understood I can't do anything without Christ.

24. Marrying the Right Person

I have learned in this life the second most important decision you can have is to marry someone. I can't state to you enough of how important this is. This is because marriage can be a blessing or a curse in your life. You can find a person who will help you to blossom, to grow in life, to grow in faith and share all the good and the bad with you, exactly how God intended marriage to be, or you can find a person who will torture you everyday of your life, driving you away from your faith, family and friends and keep you stuck in life.

Marriage and dating are not the same thing. When you date someone, it may last, it may not, but marriage is a long-term decision. You are literally deciding to spend the rest of your life with that person. This choice may lead you to a happy marriage, to a divorce or a life of suffering.

Do you understand now how serious this is? So when considering who to marry, you need to consider your feelings for the person, observe that person rationally, observe his/her behaviors and above all, pray and pray a lot, asking for direction from the Holy Spirit if that person is the right person or not.

Do not focus on human standards. Please don't. There are a lot of people carrying a church card member in their wallet who don't have a genuine relationship with Christ. They are at church every Sunday and know many Bible verses, but, ultimately, this doesn't mean they are actually Christians. So, please, pay attention if the Holy Spirit is giving you peace when you are with that person or not. The Bible says the peace of Christ should be the ruler in your heart. And pray for this matter.

Ultimately, it is better to waste a dress and a cake than waste your whole lifetime with the wrong person. All persons I have known who ended up in an abusive and terrible marriage, have said God warned them in various ways, but they just refused to listen. So, please open your ears to the Spirit.

25. The Boat of Marriage

One of the things I have learned in this life is that marriage is like a boat. This boat is not just any boat. It doesn't fit your or his/her parents, it doesn't fit your relatives, and again, it is a customized boat made for you and your spouse only. On the day of your wedding, you will both get in the boat and leave the port in order to start this new adventure.

When you start to navigate life together, there will be the soft breeze, the beautiful sunsets, the sunny days, the rainbows in the sky after rain, all those happy days, but there will also be stormy days and gray skies too.

Before you realize, there you are, navigating uncharted waters. You learn things together and deal with differences together, but the point is you are not alone. You have someone in this boat with you. That's the whole point of marriage, having someone to face the happy and tough days by your side.

Yes, this boat was made for you and your spouse; you are together, but not abandoned in the middle of the storm. God will be there with you and for you in the journey of life.

26. Relationship Dynamics Change

Following this train of thought, one of the things I have learned in this life is that relationships change with time. Being with your spouse, children, etc, relationships assume a different form. It doesn't mean you don't love the person anymore, just the relationship now has a different dynamic.

Movies tend to romanticize real life. In the movies your hair is perfect all the time, you are always well dressed, your house is well decorated, and sparkling clean and you cook like a famous French chef.

This could be the reality of the beginning of your married life, but we know it all changes when you have kids. You are not two anymore, now you became four, five or six in the boat. Walking holding hands as a couple suddenly is in the past. Having a perfect hair day is probably in the past. Eating healthy at the right time, probably not happening. Your private moments as a couple become like a secret mission, but you don't give up trying because you still love the person who is on the boat with you.

The same happens with our children. The relationship you have with your baby is one, but that baby will become a toddler, and before you blink, your cute toddler will be running in the store, throwing a tantrum because you are not going to give them, the lollipop they wanted. They will grow up and behave better but other challenges will come such as to keep them away from screens, or prevent them from spending so much time on videogames and dealing with school relationship issues. It is all wonderful, hard and scary. Your child is growing and your relationship is evolving.

As much as we miss the early days of our marriages, the impeccable homes and outfits, or the times our babies used to be small, in our arms all the time, smiling to us, waving at us and looking at us as if we were the most beautiful thing created in this world, we need to remember life is dynamic and as that's the beauty of it. In each phase, there will always be new challenges, with different types of joy and experiences.

27. Having a Child

While some people are surprised about getting pregnant because it was unexpected, the majority of us decide to get pregnant or not. In my opinion, this is the third most important decision you can make in your life. We should not get pregnant because we feel pressured to have a child or because everyone around us has a child; we should get pregnant because we want to have a child.

When you decide to have a child you need to understand your life will change a lot. You won't have the free time you had before it, you won't have the free life you had before it and if you want to be a good parent you know you will need to work hard for it.

I have seen people having kids who did it due to social pressure or to fit in, and sometimes the kids end up suffering with absent, selfish, non-caring, resentful or bitter parents. Having a child is a selfless decision. It is not about you anymore, it is about someone else. It is a decision that carries a great responsibility.

28. The Greatest Honor on This Earth

On the other hand, having a child is one of the greatest honors a human being can have. Imagine that. God is trusting you to love, nurture, teach and raise a decent human being; a baby who will be a God-fearing person and be a light in this world with so much darkness in it. It is like God is choosing you to be their angel on this Earth. You are going to kiss every boo boo, help them to stand up when they fall, help them learn to read and write and teach and advise them about this life. Can you think about a job that is so honorable like this? I just can't.

It is a lifelong job. You will be connected forever with this child. Our selfish world and society tells us when they turn eighteen, they are not our responsibility anymore. And legally they aren't, but our jobs are not done when our children leave the home. Our kids can go through difficulties in adulthood too. They can get sick, lose a job, need an extra pair of hands during some occasions in life, and we need to be there for them. Because if we are not there for them, who will it be?

And I am not talking about keep treating your kids like babies forever and not let them grow, but I am talking about we need to be in their corner when they need help, when they need advice, someone to listen to them or to pray for them.

I know it is hard to be a parent. It can be a 24/7 job, especially when the kids get sick and you can't sleep during the night. I get you. I have already cried of exhaustion before, I know what this is. But don't lose sight God chose you to be light and salt in the life of your children; to be the one who points them to Christ and be the one who will help them in times of need. This is a privilege and not a burden.

29. Dealing with Expectations

Another thing I have learned in this life is to deal with **expectations**. I have my faults as a person, but I know I am a good friend. If you are a friend, you can call me in the middle of the night and I am going to pick up the phone. I know I will do everything I can to help a friend, but I have learned that it is not because I helped a friend that this friend will be there for me if I need help.

My mom always said we know if a person is a true friend when we are in need and this is the truth. True friends don't leave you when you are going through a hard time. Real friends stay and try to do everything they can to help you. It is easy for people to be friends with you when you are helping them and everything is fine in your life, but you will know your real friends when the tough days come.

I can tell you in my 50 years I have experienced good surprises. People I didn't know would be there for me were actually there for me. I also found some friends who didn't show up in times of need, or "friends", who just disappear when they don't need you anymore. This is one of the things in life that hurts you. You feel used like a disposable paper cup.

So, since I can't change people, I changed my expectations. I do have friends and I am still a good friend, but, today, for me, friendship became a way to serve God. I see friendships as a way to serve God and people. I still expect my friends to be faithful and remain in my life, but if the person leaves because they don't need me anymore it still hurts, but I understand my mission was completed. That's the way I have learned to deal with my expectations.

And this goes for everything in our lives. We cannot do things for our children because we expect them to return the favor when we are old. We cannot love our spouse because he or she will be around when things don't look good. We give love because God wants us to love people and we serve others because we are called to do so. One thing I can tell you, though. God sees everything you do. He sees all the love you have given, and how your hand has always been open to help people around you. In the tough days, if people fail you, God will find a way to help you. It doesn't matter how, He will find a way to help you.

30. What Really Matters

I finally learned what matters in life. Every phase in my life I had different thoughts about life. When I was a child my dream was to have all the toys a child could dream and be able to eat all the candy of the world! I know I loved my family but my dream was really about toys and sweets.

When I became a teen, my dream was to be the popular girl, the one all the guys fell for and the one all the girls wanted to be friends with. I wanted a love story like the teen movies.

When I became a young adult, it was all about my career. I wanted the job of my dreams. I wanted a million dollars before my thirties, and if it could go together with a husband and kids, even better.

Today I am turning 50 and a lot of water has been under this bridge. Today my dreams are different and even happiness has a different meaning to me. Happiness to me is to connect with God and the people around me. Being rich for me now is to be healthy and alive, also being surrounded by people I love. Having my prayer time, Bible study time, my writing time, cooking a good homemade meal for my people and serving others.

Being rich for me is to be able to cook with the colorful peppers I planted and spend time with family. This is rich for me. This is priceless for me. Money is important, career is important, possessions are nice sometimes, but nothing fills my heart more than to connect with the One who created me and the ones He put in my life. We chase so many things in this world, but usually the most important things are right in front of us.

31. Called To Serve

Serving people is a great way to live this life. I grew up with my mother telling me a Brazilian saying, "Who is not good to serve is not good to live." It means if you are not here to serve others, why are you here? This saying here and there comes to my mind. Life is usually so heavy, and it is so good when we can bless someone and make this person's day a better day.

Years ago, my husband started to say to God he wanted to serve Him. His work schedule was so hectic it would be hard for him to do it at church, but God heard his sincere prayer. We always carried this jumper cable in the trunk of our car and later on that month wherever we parked there was someone whose battery was dead. My husband always helped them and said, "God bless you." It was a simple but also a good way to serve God. We felt good helping families who didn't know what to do at that moment.

I love to serve in the church but you don't need to have a position in the church to serve God. Wherever you go you are His servant. You can help someone or serve someone. Serving people is a way to serve God.

God is so perfect in His planning. You don't have to go to a far place to find people to love and serve. Yes, missionaries are sometimes called by God to go far away to share about His love, but if we are not called to go abroad to preach the gospel, all we need is to love our neighbors. Can you imagine if we all did this? If we cared about our coworkers, neighbors, and people around us in general, this world would be a better place. If each one of us took care of our neighbors, the whole world would be far better.

So if you are not following a very specific calling in the kingdom, you don't need a special preparation or course to serve God. All you need is to know your Bible and have a genuine relationship with God and it all will fall into place.

I remember a friend once asked me to pray for a specific situation that was not happening. Things seemed to be stuck. We prayed and the doors were opened. She thanked me, saying my prayers were powerful. I thanked her for the compliment, but I told her it wasn't me. It was God who solved it.

Serving is an act of love, a love that goes beyond words and feelings. Serving God, given the time, becomes such a natural thing. It is like brushing your teeth or having breakfast. God will put people in your life who need help; you will help them and give the glory to God. It is simple like this.

32. Saying Yes and No

One of my big life challenges has been the right timing to say yes and the right timing to say no. This is difficult. Sometimes people ask you something in a way it is hard to say no and you feel compelled to say yes. But being a person who had difficulty to say no I can tell you something, you can't say yes to everything and everyone. It is simply impossible.

So, once you realize this, you need to learn to be honest about what you can and can't do. Years ago when I was preparing to cook a Christmas brunch for my family, a friend called, She was crying a lot, away from home and having some not so good thoughts. The meal ingredients were on the table, but I knew my friend was too desperate and she needed someone to talk to.

I took a deep breath; put my ingredients back in the cabinet and spent the next two hours on the phone with her. I do remember we prayed for God to send her friends to the city she was in. We laughed some at the phone and at the end of the conversation she was laughing and calmer. God was so good and heard our prayers. She really made new friends in the city she was in.

I know I lost brunch with my family that day, but that phone call couldn't wait. I knew I couldn't say no to her, so I cancelled my plans in order to help my friend. Had she been calmer, if that phone call could wait, I would have told her we could do this another time.

I honestly became good at it after some time. I usually plan all the days of my week, it helps a lot to have your days planned and when something happens you have to decide how urgent it is or if it can wait.

We need to understand as much as we want to help, you cannot do everything people want all the time. It has to be doable for you too. I have known a couple pastors who have been going through depression and anxiety because they gave themselves to others so much they came to the point there was nothing left. They ended up getting sick and if you get sick you can't help anyone.

Before saying yes or no to something, we need to pray and consider all things. Years ago, I was invited to a birthday party and when I got there it was really not my cup of tea. The songs, the conversations, and the atmosphere were not what I envisioned at all. The only joy of the night was going back home. So before saying "yes" to something, we need to pray.

We need to pray for invitations and partnerships. I can't stress to you enough how serious a partnership is. Not everybody who says they are Christians, are actually Christians, so pray before you sign a contract. The same before you promise something to someone. Sometimes you can get trapped in a bad situation because you gave your word. So, please pray before saying yes or no.

33. It Is All About Balance, Balance, Balance.

One of the big challenges of our lives is to find balance in all we do. This is actually one of the greatest difficulties of the human race, especially in this generation. Having a balanced life means you are able to watch one hour of TV instead of five. It means everything is going to have some space in your life. You are going to make time for work or study, to seek God in prayer, worship, for your loved ones, for preparing meals, exercising, serving your neighbor, cleaning the house and having some entertainment too.

I know it seems impossible and I know some people have jobs which are very time consuming, but honestly, if we plan our days and focus on the daily/weekly planning it can get better.

Think about our parents' and grandparents' generation. Our grandparents didn't have video streaming or cable TV. If they had a TV, the networks stopped broadcasting at midnight and they had nothing to do but go to sleep. They didn't have smartphones, tablets, internet or social media. They had discipline. It means there was time to have breakfast, go to work, wash the car, clean up the house, say their prayers and go to sleep.

Today with all the technology and distractions, we are living in a self indulgent generation. We do what we want, when we want and look at how things are today. Kids can't get off the screens, Teens and honestly even adults can't stop playing video games. Others can't stop drinking, or exercising or watching TV, etc. The list goes on and on.

If we are honest, we are going to say for many, modern life is a mess. Instead of having time for everything, we are focusing on a couple things and all the rest gets pushed aside. I know it is not easy to juggle so many activities that happen in our lives and the unexpected things too. But at some point we have to stop and ask ourselves, how can we make our lives better?

Honestly, I understand why we do something so much and others not at all. The things we do most bring us some sort of comfort. It means instead of cleaning the bathrooms we are going to watch a show. Watching a show puts us in our comfort zone and makes us forget our frustrations and concerns. I get that, but after you watch that show for hours and hours, the bathrooms will still need to be cleaned. Did you understand how we got here?

There is a song from the eighties called "The Sun Always Shines on TV," and this is so true. On TV, everyone is successful, they never get hurt or sick, and action movie characters escape from hundreds of bullets without a single scratch. In real life, we have to deal with frustrations, problems at work, issues at home, bills to pay, doctors appointments, etc.

Entertainment doesn't solve our problems. They are still there. The house still needs to be cleaned, the kids still need to be taught and, yes, you will have to tell your children again to brush their teeth. But this is our life.

The joy we have from entertainment is an illusion. While we find refuge in entertainment, we forget about the problems, and also miss life itself. The time you call a friend or spend with your family. A special meal to share at dinner... Connection with God... Or finally being able to read a chapter of that book. While you are numb, your life is being taken from you. And I hate to say this to you, but you will never get back this time.

I am not against entertainment, but at some point we need to stop and ask ourselves how balanced our lives are. What are the things we are doing too much and what can we do to fix it. With so many distractions in this era this is a challenge for all of us. So one of the things I have learned in this life, we need to continue seeking for a balanced life. And this is not just about time management, but about all areas of our lives.

34. Focus More on Grace Than on Sin.

I have been a Christian since I was born. I was blessed growing up in the church environment around people who always helped me to grow in so many aspects. Being a person who was born in the church about fifty years ago, I can tell you I have seen the church changed in many aspects, some for better, some for the worse.

When I was a kid, I heard a lot about sin. "You are a sinner, you sinned, you sin and you will sin again." So wherever we went there was the *sin talk*. It was as if the church had this obsession about sin. It is not that they were wrong, because we are sinners, but I don't know why people only preached about sin so much and so little about God's love, mercifulness and grace.

But what I came to realize is, the more you talk and think about sin the more you sin. Because your actions are driven by your thoughts, so if you are thinking about sin all the time, there is a bigger chance you are going to… sin. But on the other hand, if you think about God's love and think about His grace and favor, it will occupy your mind in a way you will naturally feel inclined to obey God. We want to please someone who does us so much good day-after-day, don't we? So filling our minds with God's love and promises play an important role in our daily Spiritual lives.

Yes, we are sinners. We need to acknowledge our sins, confess them and pray for forgiveness, but if we think about this all the time, there is a chance we will end up sin more.

So, confess your sins, pray for forgiveness but keep the focus on the goodness of God, on His love, grace and His promises.

35. Leave the past Behind

– God's forgiveness and healing.

One thing I have learned in this life, it doesn't matter how hard you try, you will hurt God and people. As humans, we have two natures inside of us- the Godly nature and the sinful nature. The Godly nature was given to us when we were created. That's why the Bible says we look like Him. But since Adam and Eve ate the fruit, we all changed and now have a sinful nature.

When we do good things and are capable of loving someone and putting others' interest above us, it is God's nature flowing in us. However, when we sin, when we hurt, when we are selfish is the sinful nature talking and flowing in us.

Do you know what my biggest dream is? To be perfect. Yep. That's my biggest dream. Not to be arrogant but simply because I hate disappointing God and people in general. And as much as I hate it, I know here and there I am going to end up hurting God and my fellow human beings.

Sin is a crazy thing. You are doing okay with God and people around you and suddenly you look like an airplane that was hijacked, doing things that don't look like you.

I know it is terrible. As I always say, "sin is ugly" because it is. The embarrassment comes, the shame, the desire to go back in time and do things differently, but you can't.

The Bible says our story doesn't end there, though. Because of a Loving God, who loves us deeply, we can confess our sins, repent and ask for His forgiveness. The Bible says if we do that He will not only forgive you but will also purify us.

The Bible tells us God throws our past sins to the bottom of the sea. Do you know how deep the depth of the sea is? Nobody can reach it because it is so deep. Like Paul says in the Bible, we should leave the past in the past and look ahead. Here and there you will find people who will point fingers at you and bring the past back to the surface to make you feel smaller, less worthy, less everything, but if you repented and asked for forgiveness, don't fall for it, you were forgiven and a new chance was given to you.

But what if you are not the one who sinned? What if you are the one who has been hurt? Then, you need to be healed, and healing also comes from the Lord. God doesn't want you living and walking with an open wound, He wants to heal you. God can not only heal your body, but He can also heal your heart and soul. The same way we ask for forgiveness when we hurt people, we can ask for healing when we are hurt.

God is the key for us to leave the past behind, as ones who hurt or the ones who were hurt.

36. You Should Embrace the Moment

If you are nostalgic, your mind will always find comfort in thinking about the past or remembering the good times you've had - Maybe the times your kids were little, the times their hands could fit inside yours, or the good times with people who are away or are gone. I get it. Some people still are living in the past because of the comfort it brings or still reliving the same old pain or hurt.

Others are living in the future. They can't wait to have the house of their dreams or finish college or start a new professional project or find their special someone. Some are not focused on the present because they are worried about the future. The future looks like a giant question mark and this terrifies them. They can't stop thinking about the job they have to perform the next day or the test they are going to have at school. They just can't stop worrying about all those things.

Living in the past or concerned about the future steals the joy of the moment we are living. There is a reason this day, which we are living in, is called "Present," because that's what it is, a gift from God. When we are too anxious for the future or locked in the past, you can't appreciate the day the Lord gave you.

When I was young I saw the majority of my friends getting married, having kids, getting engaged, but it didn't happen to me. What did I do then? I said to myself while those things didn't happen I was going to use my time to serve God.

So, that's what I did. At one church, I was a Sunday school teacher and at another church I sang on the worship team. I've sung in the choir, preached, led prayer meetings and small groups or life groups. I sang in a gospel rock band, went on mission trips, made friends, went to church camps, studied the Bible, etc. If I were married with kids I am absolutely sure I wouldn't have done ten percent of what I did.

Today I look back and I am so happy I had the time, condition and opportunity to serve God. I've had the opportunity to travel to places I wanted, launch my first book, record an album, go to a coffee shop to read a book and wander around the mall or book stores without having the concern to feed someone or take care of them. Those were special days and I am glad I've lived them fully.

So, even if your reality today is not what you wanted or expected, this day is still a present from God to you. I like to think in the present as a box God gave you. In this box, you have a Bible, a recipe book, arts and crafts material and so many other things. God gave you the box. What are you going to do with it?

I guess this is the secret of enjoying the present. You've already received the present, but you have to choose how well you are to use this present. What about trying a new recipe today, or calling someone you haven't talked to for a long time? How about starting a new Bible study or visiting a friend? What about checking with the church of how you can get involved? This *moment* is in your hands because this is the day the Lord gave you. You decide what to do with it.

I know we cannot hide our heads in the sand, pretending life is perfect, but you can do both. You can enjoy your moment while you pray for what hasn't happened yet.

37. There is Always a Reason for What You Are Going Through

I have always wanted to be a writer since I was nine years old. Suddenly, when I was in my teens, while deciding what major to study at the University, my friend told me she was going to study *Tourism* at the University. The course seemed so nice. I could imagine myself travelling across the globe, meeting new people, new places, etc.

As crazy as it is, in my first try, I passed on our equivalent to the SAT in Brazil and entered college shortly after, but when the classes started, day-after-day, I started questioning myself what in the world I was doing there. The following four years would be like this. I felt as if I had ruined everything. It didn't make sense at all.

In college I studied philosophy, anthropology, sociology, world culture, Brazilian culture, world geography, Brazilian history and geography, research methodology, psychology, art history, event coordination, administration, statistics, geopolitics and basics of law.

What if I told you I need all these subjects when I am writing my books? The research methodology learned is the same one I use to build my books today. When I am writing a character, I have to build them based on principles learned of sociology, psychology, etc. When I think about my books, I think this major was absolutely perfect for what I am doing today.

Yes, I am a Christian writer and I need the Bible and God's inspiration to do so, but what I have learned at college helps my books to bring extra information and insight. It is like a Christian singer, who learned by herself and others who took music classes. Both are good, but the second one may have techniques that will protect her vocal chords in the future.

There are things we are going through today that don't seem to make any sense, but later you will understand why you needed to go through them. Sometimes, we need to learn something, sometimes we need to toughen up or soften up, or sometimes it is just a blessing in disguise as it was with me. Keep trusting in God and keep walking. The journey is never in vain.

38. You Probably Won't Change the World.

When we are in our twenties, we believe we are going to change the world, don't we? We truly believe we are going to end hunger in Africa or wars in the world, etc. And yes, there are people in this world who changed the world, like Jesus, for example. Of course, according to the Bible, Jesus is the son of God and we are mortals, but there are people whose work and discoveries saved and helped millions throughout the world. Think about penicillin, for example. Before its discovery, people died from simple infections which are totally manageable these days. Can you imagine how many people died in the past because they didn't have this medicine?

So, yes, there are some people who have impacted millions of lives in a positive way, however, not all of us are going to change the lives of millions. Not all of us will have the influence or resources to change many lives, but listen to me, if you help one person you can change someone else's life.

Years ago, I was in a band. Until this day I don't know the full impact of our music, but I know one person who accepted Christ after one of our concerts. We talked to Him about Jesus, prayed with him and he received

Christ as his savior. Two years later, he met us again to thank us for leading him to Christ. He became an enthusiastic evangelist for his church and led more than 200 people to Christ! Wow! We know it was the Spirit who touched his heart. We were simply the instrument, but that one person has led hundreds to Christ.

People have no idea how hard a band works to produce a song, at least how we used to do it at that time. Hours of rehearsals, meetings, tests, trips and prayers. It was a lot of time consuming work. But you know what? I would do it all again if it meant being an instrument which would lead that one person to Christ. And then he ended up sharing the gospel with so many others.

Sometimes people try to diminish what you do because of your results, but you will never know how many lives you actually touch with what you do. What you do for Christ matters, what you do to help others matters too. Keep this in mind.

39. Your Life Won't Go As You Planned

Graduated at 22; dream job at 23; married at 24; car paid off; house paid off; first child at 27; parenthood and profession perfectly balanced, right? Eh, how can I break this to you? It probably won't happen like that. I know for some people it happens like this, but not for the majority of us.

You probably don't remember, but in the eighties there were toys which looked like a can or box, called jack in the box. When you opened them up, it could be a flower bouquet or a scary toy animal to scare you. You didn't know what was inside and you only found out after you opened it. Yep, that's life for you!

So, you may have had to postpone your education dream or it was very difficult to find the right person to marry or you or your spouse lost a job and now you have to refinance your mortgage. Maybe you have been trying to conceive a child for years and it doesn't happen or your spouse turned into a totally different person after marriage and there you are facing marital problems.

Many times we look at our lives and think "I really didn't see it coming." Yes, we didn't. Dealing with plans which are crushed and shattered dreams are not easy. It may lead someone to become a frustrated and bitter person.

Once a pastor told me, our life is like a tree, if we put our list of plans in the root, we are going to be disappointed, because guess what? We can't control the tree. We can't control how far the tree is going to grow, how much fruit it will yield, or what direction the branches grow. But if we put God in the root of that tree, we will understand the branches are going in the direction He wants to, such as the fruit is growing like He wants. We will understand the fruit given to us came from God's hand and even if this fruit is not what we expected, we understand it came from God to us.

Putting God in our tree's root is surrendering our tree to Him. It means you trust He will do the best for you, even if the best is not what you expected.

When we face the plans which didn't happen and shattered dreams, there are only two ways for you to go- you are going to submit yourself to the Lord or you will rebel from Him. And I have seen both.

God gives you the freedom to make your decisions every day. You are free to rebel against Him or accept His teaching. So, as I said before, I have seen people choose both ways, but one thing I can observe, the people who rebel against the Lord seem to be stuck in many ways, while those who accept His teachings, grow. It doesn't mean they became millionaires or have a boat, it means they grew as Christians, as humans and became more compassionate and humble. This is because when we submit ourselves to the Lord, our struggles make sense in the end.

40. Be Thankful

It doesn't matter how much you accomplish in this life, you will always have someone to thank. There's no such thing as a "self-made" man or woman. We made it to where we did it due to someone helping us on the way.

Think about it. You came into this world naked, defenseless and incapable of taking care of yourself. If you didn't have someone to change your diapers, you probably wouldn't have survived. If people didn't feed you, you wouldn't have made it. I cringe when I see people with a smirk on their faces saying, "I am a self-made man."

How did you learn to read again? And multiply? Oh, you had a teacher who taught you to read, write and work with numbers. What about the sports medals you won at school? Oh, there was a coach who helped you, taught you how to play the game and prepared you to win.

At this point, I am afraid you already know where I am heading. We got where we are today because somebody had our backs on the way. Nobody is dismissing your effort, believe me, but you didn't get to the place you are today by yourself.

When I think about this, my heart gets full of gratitude for the Lord Himself and for the people the Lord has sent into my life. I remember my teacher who taught me to read and write, and because of that woman, today I write books. I remember all my Sunday school teachers who taught me about God, Jesus and the Holy Spirit. The church pastors I have been part of throughout my life, men who were absolutely committed to serve God and people.

I think about my parents who taught me so many precious lessons, which I pass onto my kids. I also think about my friends, acquaintances and even random people who gave me a tip about a recipe, etc. Each one of these people helped me during my life.

In other cultures, we have the habit to honor those who helped us and I wish we did this instead of having a culture which stimulates us to elevate ourselves. The good news is it's never too late to thank the people who helped you to get where you are today.

What about God then? According to the Bible, He created us, sustains us, and provides us all things we need to live. He sent His Son to rescue and save us. We live in a society that pushes us to be constantly unsatisfied, so we can buy more, spend more and keep looking for the things we don't have. Do we recognize all God has done for us? Are we thankful enough?

Gratitude happens when we are able to see what we have and don't focus on what is missing. Can we see what God is doing for us on a daily basis? Can we see what people are doing for us? How can we thank them? How can we show appreciation for God and people's goodness toward us? We need to ask ourselves these questions so we can change our perspective and act in a more grateful way.

41. Eat the Cheesecake

A couple months ago my sister in law and I were in a fancy coffee shop. They had a cheesecake that cost an arm and a leg and we were debating if she should buy the fancy cheesecake. I told her, "You know what? Get the cheesecake. We never know for how long we are going to be able to do this, so please eat the cheesecake." She got the cheesecake and she loved it!

I know many of you are reading and thinking we were overreacting, but bottom line, we weren't. Everything can change in a blink of an eye. What if, God forbid, my sister in law could not eat sugar anymore or became lactose intolerant? She would never be able to try the cheesecake then. I've known people who waited their whole life to retire so they could travel, but when they retired, they couldn't take the trip anymore due to health issues.

In 2019 I remember our whole family was going to make a photo session and my mom convinced us not to do it. We were going to spend money and she was not very enthusiastic to do this. We would have to go to a studio, there was the logistics to get there and we ended up not doing it. My mom's health declined so much since then and I now regret not doing it. Those perfect photos of my mom and her grandchildren never came true and now she is not able to do it anymore.

We need to keep this in perspective when opportunities come around. I've come to know so many people who saved every penny and when they get old they regret having the money, but not the memories. The energy and health are gone. So do what you can while you can.

42. Do What You Can With the Resources You Have

Let's suppose you want to go to the Bahamas, but you can only afford to travel to the beach in your state. You can go to the closer beach, then! Or you would like to go to the beach, but you can't afford it. You have enough money to put gas in the car and take your kids to a splash pad at the park. It sounds good! Oh, you would like to get married in a castle dressed like a princess, but you only have the means to have a simple ceremony at your home. Why not at home, then?

Sometimes we wait for the perfect condition and circumstance to do the things we want, but the perfect condition may never arrive, so we need to do what we can with the resources we have.

The pandemic was a real wake up call for me. After you have kids, you are so busy that it is easy to postpone plans. I wanted to go back to writing, I wanted to serve in the church, but I always postpone it for the next year, or for the next six months. So when the pandemic hit and all those people started passing away, I realized maybe there wouldn't be a "later." I knew I had all these books in my heart and knew I had to make it happen.

Honestly, it wasn't easy. I had to write when the kids were sleeping or when my husband could watch the kids so I could focus on my writing. But almost six years later, by the grace of God, I continue writing and producing materials to inspire people.

So, do your best with the resources you have.

43. Fight for the Right Thing

God is a loving-merciful forgiving God, but God also doesn't like injustice going on in this world. Sometimes God will put you in a situation for you to fight for what is right. Honestly, it is not my favorite thing when God puts me in a situation like this. I am not a person who likes conflicts and arguments, but sometimes God calls you to fight for the right thing.

Years and years ago, I was riding the bus in the city I used to live and I saw the bus collector charging double price from tourists, since they didn't know what the right price was. I didn't say a word, but kept looking very seriously at him as if I was telling him I knew what he was doing. He then called the people and said he made a mistake and returned the money to them. I know the man was not happy with me, but I knew I had done what God wanted me to do.

Right now, while we are talking about this, there are people suffering persecutions and threats for doing what is right. Lawyers, for instance, who faced large corporations in courts, people who have faced a huge amount of pressure because they were called to do what is right.

This doesn't mean God wants you to pick a fight about everything. On the contrary, God wants us to keep the peace wherever we go, but here and there God will call you to stand up for what is right.

It is not a comfortable place to be at, but sometimes God will put us in a place because He wants us to help make things right. You may lose friends in the process, but bottom line, this is between you and God.

44. Try Something New

This life is a gift, a present God gave you so you can learn and grow. It is a journey and you should take the best out of it. Imagine you are going to a huge and famous amusement park. They have tons of attractions, but you decide you are only going to spend the whole day at the carousel; you are not even going to take a walk around the park or try another attraction. You are going to be at the carousel the whole day, over and over again until the park is closed.

As much as you love the carousel, that's all you did! You didn't explore the park, you didn't try any other attractions; you just stayed there. Sometimes this can be us living our lives. You have so many things to learn and explore in this world, healthy things, hobbies, knowledge, but there you are doing the same thing over and over again.

No wonder people are so discouraged lately. There is nothing new going on. You are not trying to learn anything new or grow and keep doing the same of the same day after day. How could it be any different with you living your life like this?

There come the excuses, "I don't have time." Do you have a break at work? Lunchtime? Do you watch TV every night? So, I think you still have a little bit of time. "I don't have money," Many people do things with little to no resources at all.

There are free online courses at universities you can take - courses about administration, art history, or poetry. There are online courses like graphic design and others for not much cost. We are in the middle of an information revolution. There's so much to learn. One course per year, two books per year and a new hobby here and there.

There are so many courses about the Bible, so many interesting new books to read, new things you can do at your church. I have learned how important it is to try to learn something new. This year I started a tiny garden. It is so impressive to see life growing with tiny peppers blossoming in different colors.

I know I won't become a millionaire because I tried something new, but I will learn something new, something to widen my horizons and perspective about God and life.

45. A Joyful Heart

The Bible says the joy of the Lord is our strength. Do you know what it means? When we receive this joy from the Lord it makes us stronger. Every day there is bad news in this world and difficult people around us, but we cannot allow these things to steal our joy. If we allow these things to put us down, we are going to be weaker, discouraged and hopeless.

Yes, we need to know what is going on around us and in this world. We cannot live in fantasy land. We need to deal with frustrations, disappointments, and comparisons, but remember, nobody is you or has the same journey you do. So, please don't let these things steal the sparkle in your eyes. You are still alive and still have things to be thankful for.

Sometimes we are around people who are bitter, hopeless, frustrated, and ungrateful as nothing is ever good to them and it's hard not to be influenced by them. But do everything you can to keep your hopes up, keep in mind God's promises and don't let these things steal the joy God gave you.

46. Build Things in the Kingdom

This world is built on a couple of things – money, possessions, power, status, success, etc. Deep, deep inside all we want is to be loved. Bottom line, many people think for them to be loved means to find success, so they can be recognized, accepted and celebrated. Time passes and one day, whatever you have built in this world will be forgotten.

I remember when I was a child in the eighties there was this musical and artistic scene in Brazil like never seen before. It is hard to put into words as I don't know if this will ever happen again. The record labels were everywhere seeking for new talents as were the radio stations, TV stations, promoters, etc. It was wild. One day you had a garage band and the next day you couldn't leave home because people were asking for your autograph wherever you would go.

There was space for everyone, from rock-and-roll, pop, romantic, country, folk, MPB (Brazilian Popular Music), funk, etc. Oh my, so many styles, bands, singers and musicals. It was absolutely crazy! The same happened with soap opera actors and actresses. Those people wouldn't dare to leave their homes as there were people following them everywhere.

Years passed and here we are in 2026. What if I told you only a few of these bands are still around now? What if I told you some of them are not even remembered any longer? Many of their songs were simply forgotten.

It is all gone. Those amazing songs are now lost in time. Isn't that crazy? If you saw those people and how famous they were. If you saw people running after them, you wouldn't believe one day it would be forgotten, but it is the case. These people worked so much to build things in this world but it is all lost. Some of them are even gone by now. Their success? Gone. Their songs? Gone. All gone.

The same will happen with us one day. That's why the Bible says we should build our treasure in heaven, where it can't be destroyed. When you bless someone, help someone, worship the Lord, pray for someone, and share the hope we find in the gospel, this will all echo in God's kingdom. This will remain because God lasts forever.

We put so much of our energy on the things of this world, so much work to buy things and have more money and possessions. All this for what? One day we all will be gone and the majority of your possessions will be donated for charities or sold for pennies. The only thing which will remain according to the Bible is what we build in the immaterial world.

Yes, I am a Christian and I have heard this since when I was a kid, but seeing all these people gone, all their efforts forgotten, makes the Scripture verses real.

So, I know, we all have to pay bills and have to work, but where are we really investing our talents? This world or God's kingdom?

47. You are Not Everyone

When I was a child sometimes I became frustrated because some people were allowed to do some things and I wasn't. "Mom, can I do this? Everyone is doing it," I asked. "No. You are not everyone," My mom answered. And you know what? She was right. I don't have to do what everyone is doing simply because everybody is doing it.

I am close to my fifties and I have never smoked a cigarette in my life nor ever tried any type of substances. And you know what? I am fine. I don't need to smoke a cigarette to find out it's not good for my health. I don't need to try illicit substances to know that sometimes you can start using them, but not always you will be able to stop. In other words, I don't need to play with fire to find out I can get burnt.

I know sometimes it's not easy. Sometimes you won't be called to gatherings because you don't drink alcohol or smoke, but people who love you will love you the way you are. This sums it up.

I know a story of a businessman who used to have two or three meetings a couple days of the week. He didn't use to drink, but every time he went to a meeting, the other person wanted some companionship to have a drink while they talked business. Needless to say, this man ended up being an alcoholic, damaging his liver and ended up passing away from it.

I am not here trying to tell you how to live your life, but you should not be doing things you don't want or are not comfortable with just out of pressure.

48. God Has the Final Word

It is so hard when you are living in a situation in your life you don't see a way out. But one of the things I have learned in my life is, God is the one who has the final word about everything.

A friend of mine went to the doctor as she wanted to have a child. The doctor not only told her changes to have a child were slim to none, but she also wrote it on a prescription script. My friend left the doctor's office devastated. This could be the end of the story, but it wasn't. Oh, but how special it is to see her daughter growing and smiling. She is such a cute girl. God is an amazing Father!

A friend's sister was in the hospital. It didn't look good. She was in the ICU and her doctor called to prepare the family for the worst. My friend said to the doctor she was not God and only God could determine how long her sister would live.

We started praying for her sister, and a couple days later, she left the ICU. A couple days after that, she was discharged from the hospital. One year later, her sister is alive and well.

Bad news strikes us hard, but at these times we need to remember God has the final saying regarding everything in our lives.

49. Don't Hold More Than You Can Carry

One of the memories about my early twenties is when I was going to college, and also studying English, Spanish and German at the same time. I always loved interacting with people, communicating with new people, learning about new cultures and I absolutely loved learning a new language, new words, etc. My goal was to become a polyglot, who is a person which can communicate in many languages, so that I could interact with many cultures and people from many countries.

One day, I went to a class and suddenly the languages literally started to scramble in my mind. I was speaking in German at an English class, so I knew it was not okay. I realized going to college and studying three languages at the same time was more than I could handle at that point. I needed to rethink what I was doing or I could get burnt out mentally. Praise God, I was wise enough to not insist and was able to prioritize what I liked the most, this way I could study another language in the future.

In our lives, sometimes we want something so much we end up getting in trouble because of it. Let's suppose you want to have a large family. Should you have a large family? Can you handle it? Do you have enough stamina to do it? Will your spouse help you? Do you have a support network?

Having a large family with many kids is not for everyone. I have seen people take care of 10-child household, but I also hear the stories of moms who did the unthinkable because they were absolutely overwhelmed, exhausted and mentally drained.

I know God is with us and sometimes when you think you can only do so much, God will show you can handle more than what you think. He will make you stronger and enable you to do what you need to do. However, we need to be responsible with the activities we are going to insert into our daily routine. The day only lasts 24 hours and there is only one of you.

We need to pray before taking an extra shift at work, starting a new course or having one more baby. Each one of us has a different pace, so it is important you know yourself, and what works for you or not.

It took me some time to understand I can only do so much. I have learned to plan my weeks. In my week planner, I only write the priorities. All the rest I am going to insert them one at a time.

If it can wait, it is going to be done, but in a planned and calmer way. This way I can avoid stress and extra pressure in my daily life. I do everything I can to keep things simple and practical so you can enjoy the moment and not be too suffocated by many activities.

50. Find Your Voice

It is hard to believe, but it took me thirty years to find my voice. Having the personality of a people pleaser and a mom who raised me to be a lady (just smile and wave in a classy manner when people are going after you), it led me to struggle to speak my mind and stand up for myself.

I consider myself a very patient person. I am not judgmental, but an easy going person. I understand people are different and they have different weaknesses and they are going through their own challenges in life. So, as I said before, I am very patient with people around me, but, of course, I have my limits too. I usually take a deep breath and put up with a lot, but eventually I will reach my limit. And, then, I know I need to do something about it.

Some think Jesus allowed people to do whatever they wanted to Him, but that's not true at all. Jesus had enough when people were going to church not because of God, but because it was a nice place for commerce. And so many times in the gospels, Jesus was firm while religious people at the time tried to humiliate Him, diminish His ministry and question His authority. He always answered them in a way they didn't know how to answer Him back.

Sometimes all you need is a conversation. Sit with the person and say, "Hey, this is not good for me" or "You can't treat me like this." It worked a lot for me, and honestly, it works for many people.

Unfortunately, I understand it doesn't work for everyone. Sometimes people are living in circumstances they can't stand up for themselves, as they can't simply open the door and get out of that situation either. But, you can't lose faith and give up hope. Don't stop praying and waiting on the Lord because we believe in a God who can change people's circumstances and bless us in so many ways.

51. You are still you – The challenge of getting old

In each phase of your life, you will have challenges. When you are a baby, you will have to learn to wave, roll, crawl, walk, touch your feet, etc. When you are a child, you will have other challenges like starting school, avoid falls, control your impulses as you were taught to, etc.

Life goes fast as a blink of an eye. Suddenly, you are a teenager. Then you became an adult, where you have your first job, eventually, you get married, then have kids.

One day you will wake up different. One day you will develop back pain you didn't have before, for example. If you are a woman, menopause will arrive sometimes without a notice, leaving you confused and trying to understand what is going on.

Many people will do HRT (Hormonal Replacement Therapy), but not everyone will be suitable to do it, nor does everyone want to have HRT. Some will deal with it with supplements and some, tea herbs. Each person will search for a way to find relief.

It doesn't matter how many procedures you have had, this day will come. Suddenly, your skin won't be shiny and your hair may get overly dry. Some people will be comfortable with white hair, while some won't.

It is curious because we think getting old is a synonym for a peaceful and relaxing time. For many, the kids have left the house or are more independent and they think they will be able to enjoy slowing down and do nothing at last.

But what I found out is quite the contrary. When you are aging, you start being concerned with things you never needed before. You have to start moisturizing your hair more often, take better care of your skin, and have some vitamins and supplements. And, as much as you don't like it, you'll need to move your body, do some physical exercise in order to help your body in the aging process.

You are going to look yourself in the mirror and see some differences, but there is one thing you cannot forget of, you are still you. Even if your body is changing, you need to remember your essence remains the same. You are the same person with the same distinct features, qualities and imperfections. You are still you.

So next time you feel down for dealing with so many changes, remember this is also part of your journey and you are still yourself. Remember many people don't get the chance to reach this point of life. Be grateful and enjoy. Your life is still a gift from God and you need to make the best out of it.

52. This Too Shall Pass – A Temporary Home

While I am writing this chapter I am thinking about life and how it is frail. If you ask me about the heroes of my life, I would talk about the amazing people I had the honor to meet in this world. People who added something to my life in ways I will never forget.

My mom singing hymns to me when I was a child, helping me learn about God. My father and his precious lessons, my pastors, my Sunday School teachers, my aunts and uncles, and so many faithful women of God. These people were so strong. They looked like oak trees. They seemed indestructible and it seemed nobody could put them down.

We are now in 2026 and some of them are not even here anymore. Others are still in this world, but far from who they used to be.

Last time I was with my mother, who is 85, and sometimes having memories issues, she looked at me and said, "You are so good to me… I love you as if you were my daughter." She said and I smiled, because even she couldn't remember who I was at the moment, she loved me like a daughter and this meant the world to me.

While my heroes grow older and frail, I know what we have in this world is temporary. I know this life is a journey, a wonderful journey made of prayers, hugs, connection with God and people. It is a journey with discoveries, accomplishments; disappointments, and failures.

This life is a journey with laughter and tears which will lead us to a forever home. Jesus says in the Bible whoever believes His word and in His Father has passed from death to life. According to the Bible, our death here in this world is not the end. It is just the beginning of an eternal life.

However, while we are here, we have to do everything we can to connect to God and people, to taste this life in a responsible way, while we plant seeds in the kingdom.

It doesn't matter what stage of life we are in. There is always something to learn. And God is eager to teach us.

50 Lessons In 50 Years

Epilogue

While I write a party supplies list for my 50th birthday party, I see this book coming to an end. Writing this book has been such an incredible journey.

Every time when I am writing a Christian book, I have to think, rethink, read and reread because the Christian community is a diverse community and my goal is never to divide but keep the unity.

When I was writing the book, the Holy Spirit told me something very interesting, "If the Son sets you free, you are free indeed." This was so special to me. It was as if God was saying to me "I set you free, you are free to tell about what you've learned," and this gave me peace about this project. I do believe God wants me to write this book.

This book was not written to tell you how you should live your life. It was never the intention. Your life is your journey and nobody else's, but I wanted to share what I have learned in this life. Maybe any of the things I have learned and shared will bless your life and inspire you somewhat.

Last, my heart is full of gratitude for the Lord and all the amazing experiences He allowed me to live in these fifty years, all the amazing people He put in my life. I recognize Him all the way through.

Like the day I was on second grade and, I can't recall why, but two boys challenged me to a fight during recess and I knew I couldn't back down. I had the physique of Popeye's Olive Oil and there I was to fight those two boys. When it all started, a friend of mine showed up. She was taller and stronger than me. "What in the world is going on here?" She asked and I explained the situation. "What a bunch of cowards. Two boys fighting a girl!" She said and went after them. They ran like scaredy-cats.

Needless to say, we became best friends after that time, and we are still friends. God knew the fight wouldn't end up well for me, and *placed her there at the right time.*

Since my first breath, God was there and He will be there at my last one!

All glory to God!

Dea A. Myers

Other Titles from the Author

Inspirational Books

HOPE (We All Need It)

Never an Accident

Encouragement for the End Times

2-in-1 Book Collection

Novels

The Book of the Secrets – Book I

Hector & Amalia

Prayer Notebooks

My Prayer Requests Book

Books in Portuguese

Esperança

Released Songs

In My Father's Time

There's a Light

Questions and comments, feel free to drop us a line at
deaamyers@gmail.com